Swamp Chomp

by **Lola M. Schaefer**

illustrated by **Paul Meisel**

Holiday House / New York

In the swamp . . .
water ripples.

Mosquitoes flit. **Sit**.

Dragonflies swoop. **Dip**.

Crayfish crawl. **Carry**.

Bullfrogs wait. **Lay**.

Fish glide. **Guard.**

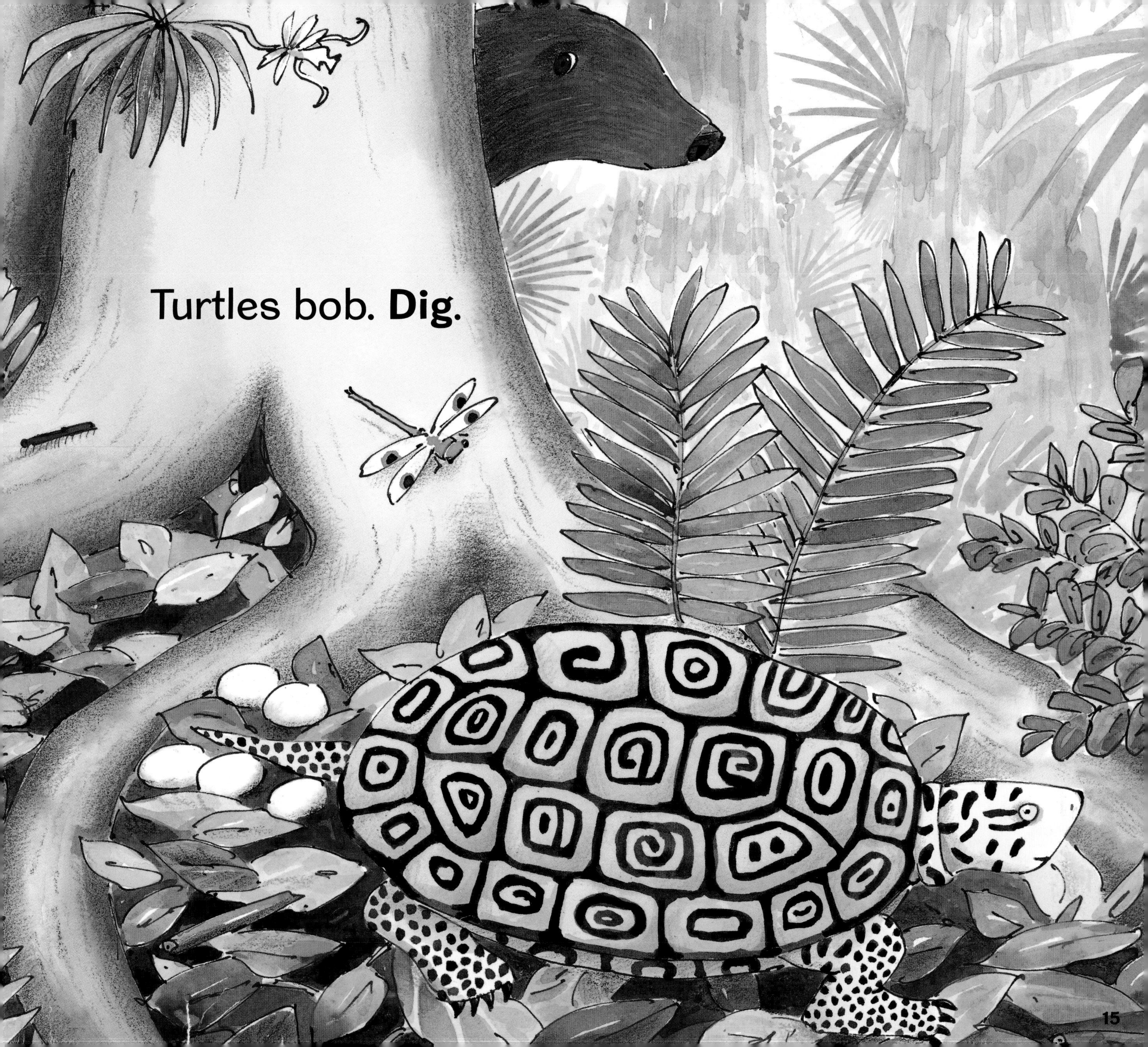

Turtles bob. **Dig.**

Eyes rise. **Watch.**

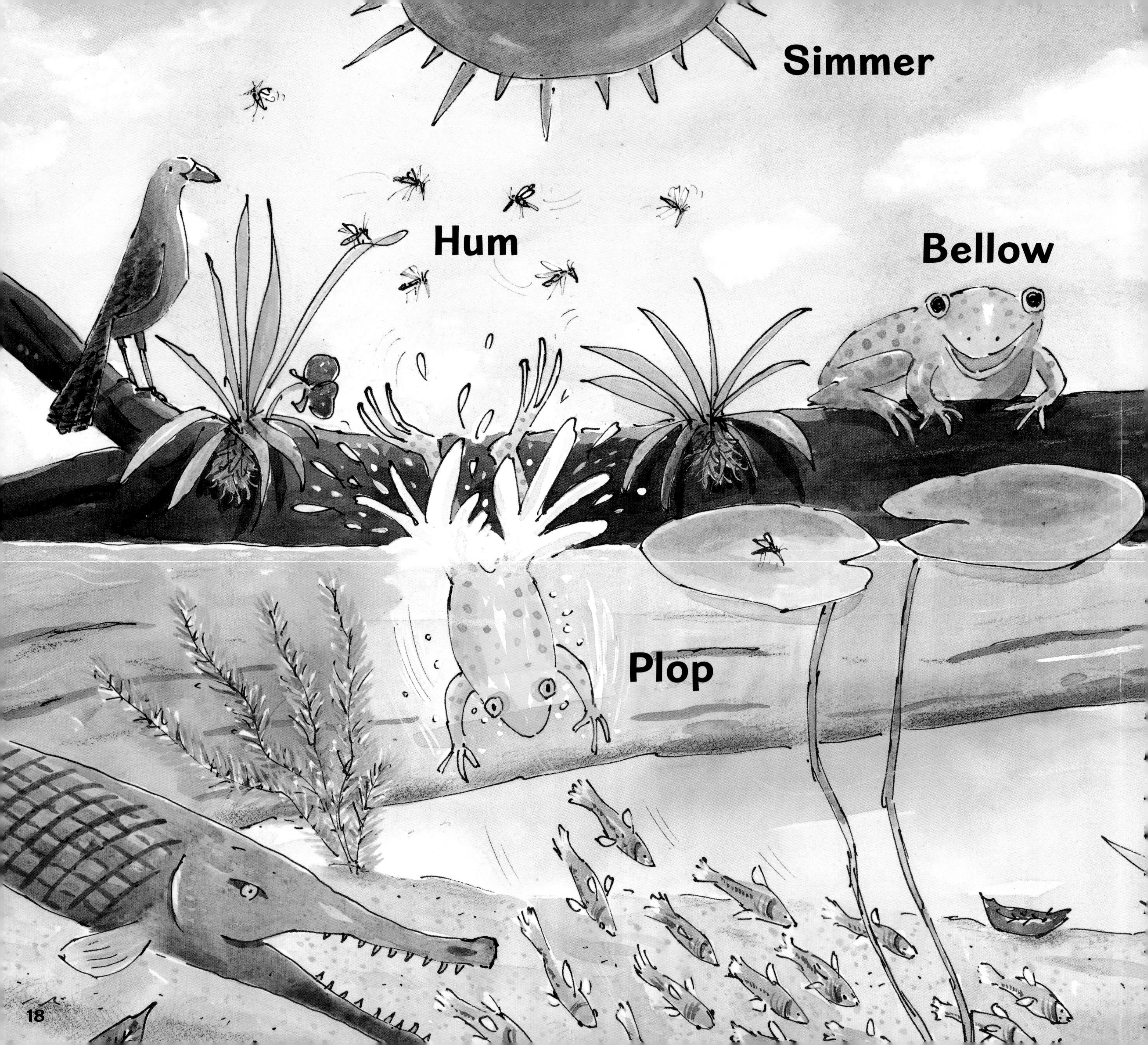
Simmer
Hum
Bellow
Plop

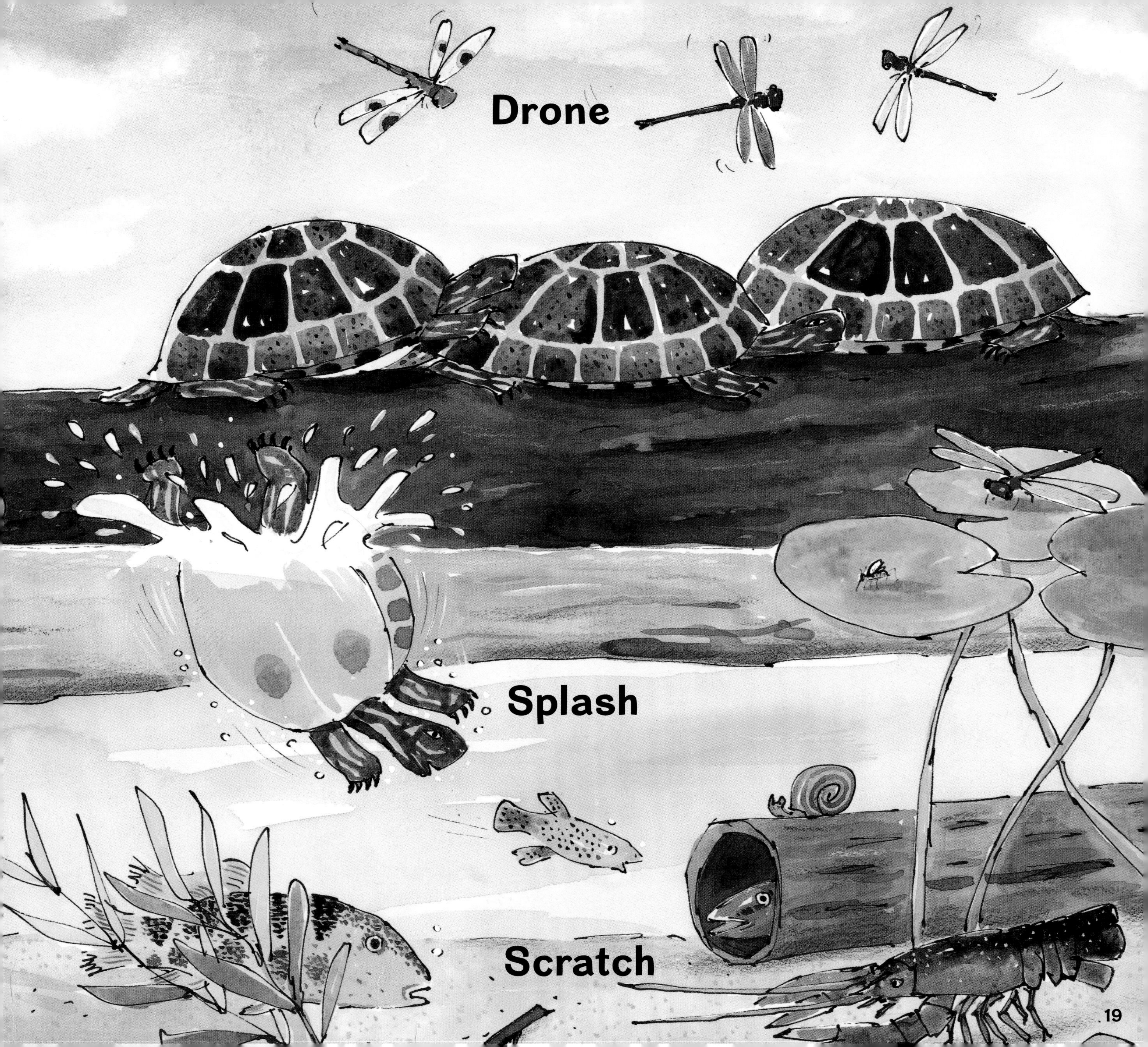
Drone
Splash
Scratch

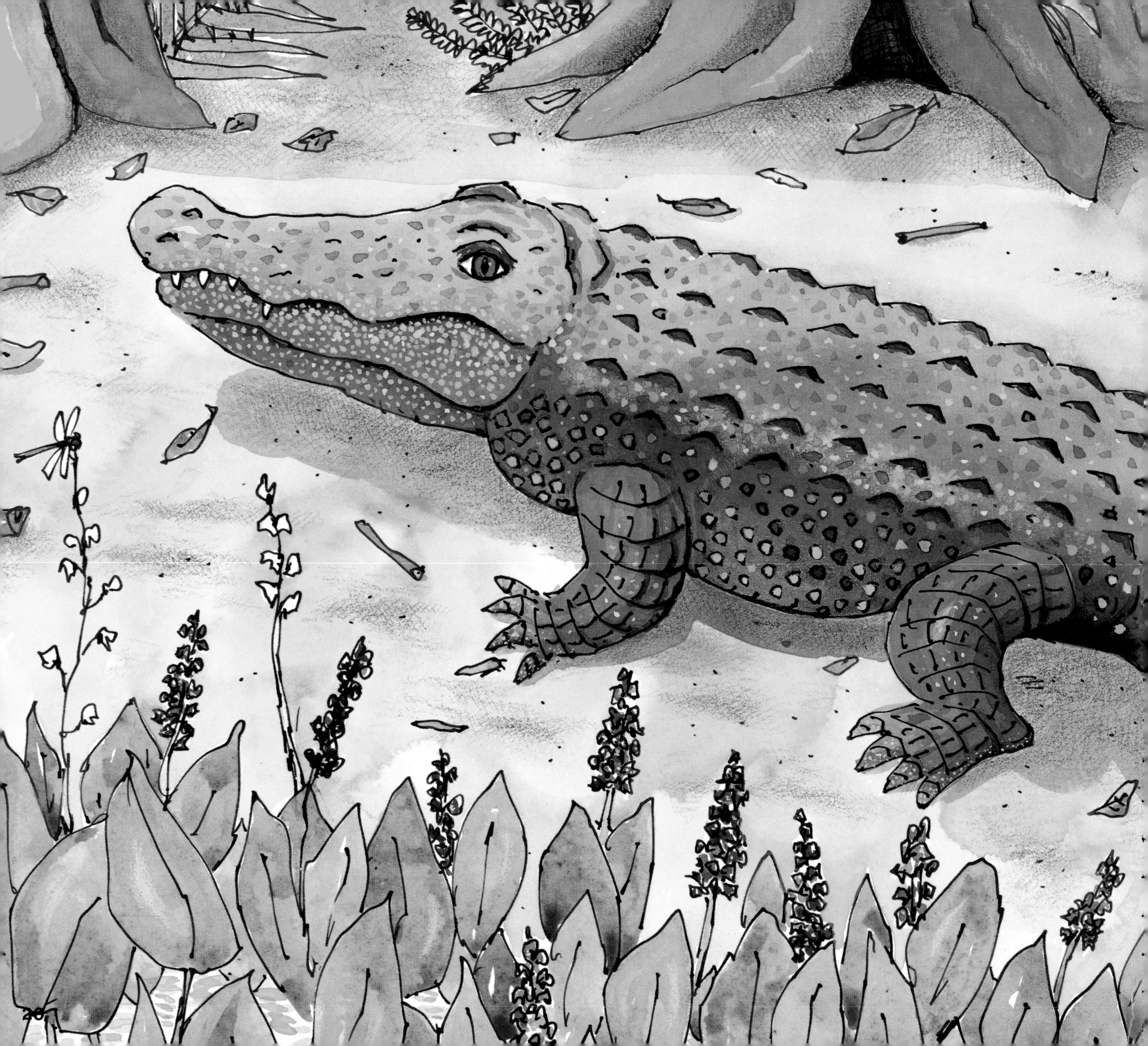

Swish

Mosquitoes land.
Nibble.

Dragonflies circle.
Slurp.

Crayfish grab.
Munch.

Bullfrogs pounce.
Gulp.

Fish jump.
Swallow.

Turtles dive.
Snap.

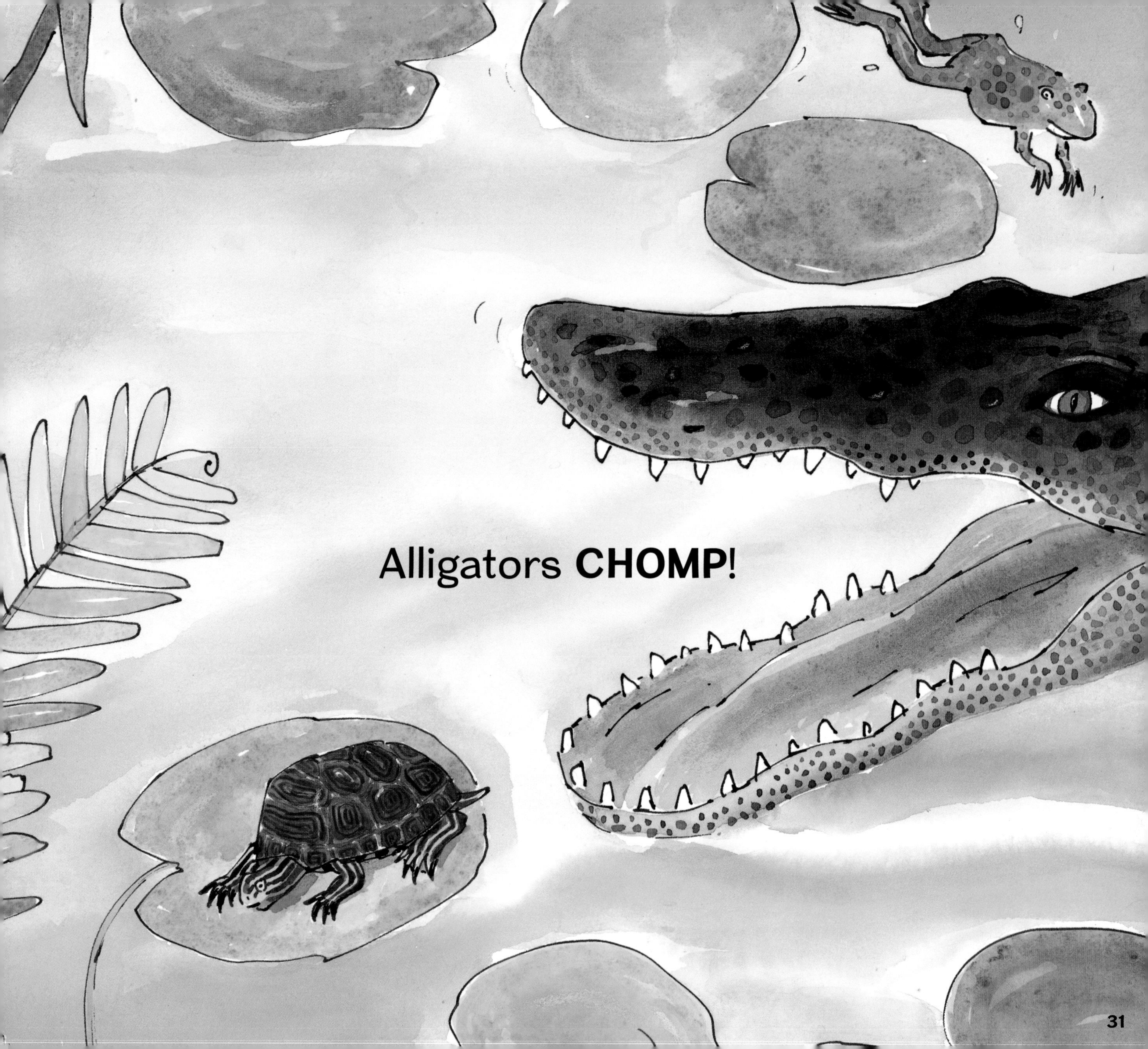

Alligators **CHOMP!**

Water ripples
in the swamp.

ENDNOTE

A swamp is a kind of wetland. Swamps hold water that moves slowly. They often flood. Many plants grow in swamps. Animals come to the swamp to eat, drink, or rest.

Plants and animals feed off one another. This way there are never too many animals or too many plants. This is called the balance of nature.

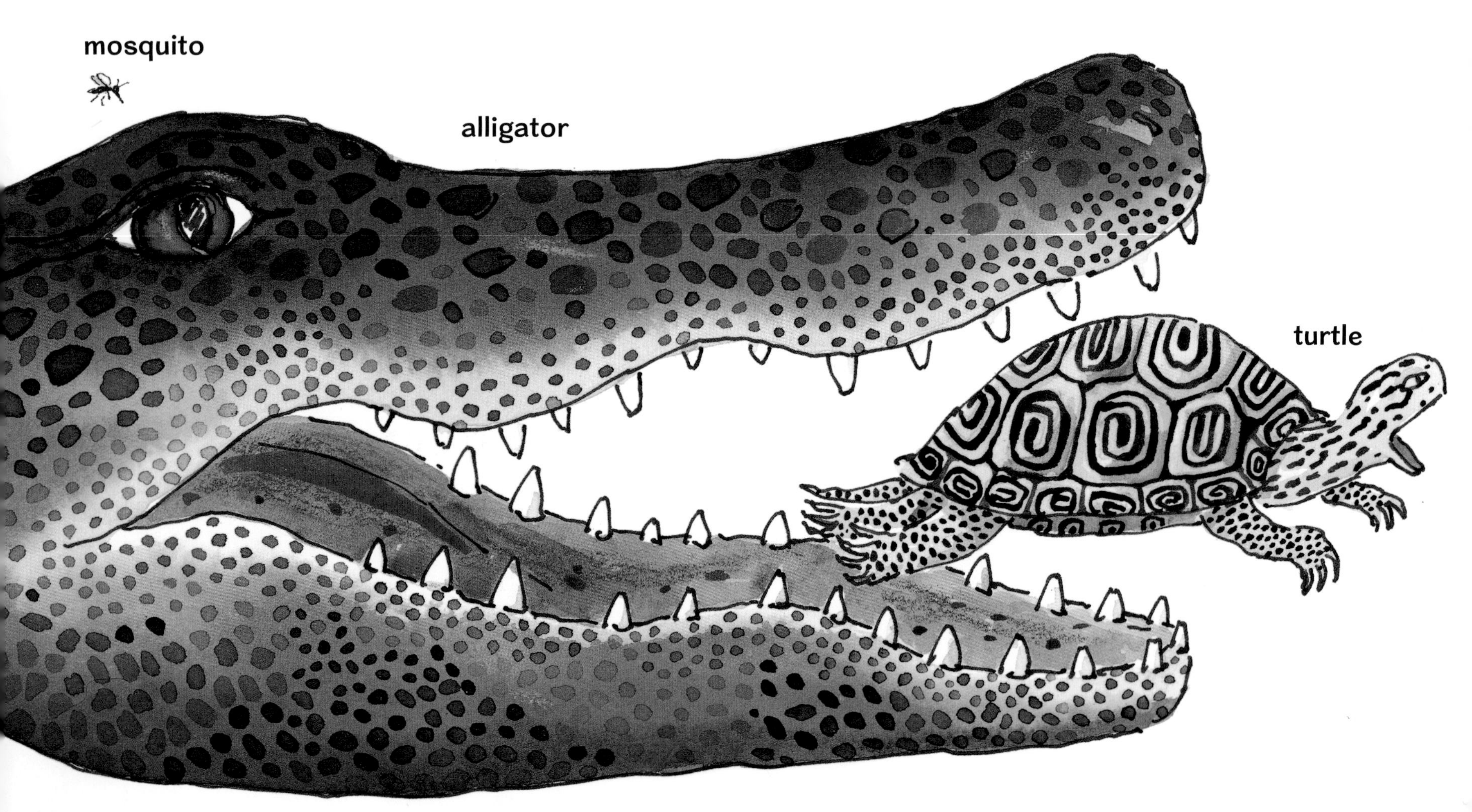

In a swamp, there are many food chains. A food chain is a chain of plants and animals that eat one another. Small creatures eat plants. Then large animals eat the small creatures.

Food chains can change. Some days there might be few animals in the swamp. Other days there might be many. The same animal doesn't always eat the very same food.

The swamp in this book is a cypress swamp. This picture shows a food chain with animals in this book.

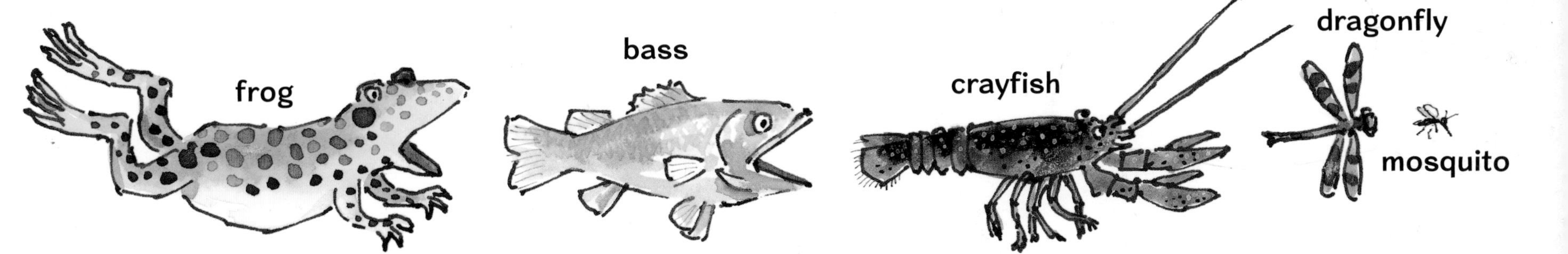

For Evianna—L. M. S.

For fellow childhood swamp adventurers Jack, Glenn, Richard, Josh, Mark, and Mickey—P. M.

**The publisher would like to thank Kathleen Sullivan Sealey, PhD,
Associate Professor, Department of Biology,
University of Miami, for reviewing this book.**

Printed and Bound in November 2013 at Toppan Leefung, DongGuan City, China.
The artwork was created with pen and ink, watercolor, acrylic, pencil, and pastel
on Arches hot press watercolor paper.
www.holidayhouse.com
First Edition
1 3 5 7 9 10 8 6 4 2

Library of Congress Cataloging-in-Publication Data
Schaefer, Lola M., 1950-
Swamp chomp / by Lola M. Schaefer ; illustrated by Paul Meisel. — 1st ed.
p. cm.
Summary: In the rippling waters of a swamp, mosquitoes fly and hum, dragonflies swoop and drone,
and other creatures live their interwoven lives. Includes facts about swamps and food chains.
ISBN 978-0-8234-2407-8 (hardcover)
[1. Swamp animals—Fiction. 2. Swamps—Fiction. 3. Food chains (Ecology)—Fiction.]
I. Meisel, Paul, ill. II. Title.
PZ7.S33233Sw 2014
[E]—dc23
2011046561